Waltzing

Through Walls

Susie Guerra and Vicki Ariatti

Waltzing Through Walls is a love story about my 6th grade English Teacher who literally changed the trajectory of my life with her unique teaching methods. She was more of a life coach and dream builder than a teacher. She gave herself to us in such a way that we became her kids and we adored her.

Mattie Miller

This book is written to share with teachers and students alike the methods and techniques that will assist in an effective teaching and learning environment.

ISBN: 978-1-7371463-0-8

Waltzing Through Walls

Special Thanks

To Irina Sztukowski for allowing us to complement our book with a beautiful image created by her on our cover.

www.artirina.com

DEDICATION

When Mattie invited me into her adult world, she gave me hope and changed my attitude completely about school, teachers, and life. This transformation became my inspiration as an adult, mother, and businesswoman.

As a direct result of knowing Mattie, my life traveled down the road less taken. This has made all the difference in who I am today.

I was an overactive child when I first sat in Mattie's class. She showed me something about myself that no one else had seen. She became my mentor and life coach. She brought out my strengths, talents, and visions that even I didn't know I possessed.

While writing this book, my heart cries with joy! So grateful that one person, Mattie Miller, my 6th grade teacher, would have the compassion and desire to give her wisdom and heart to me at such a pivotal time in my life.

This book is a love story dedicated to you Mattie! As a servant of the Lord, you waltzed into my life spreading His love with such grace and beauty. Words fall short. You continue to bless my life.

Susie and Mattie at grade school reunion

INTRODUCTION

Mattie Miller was catapulted into our lives like a flaming arrow as she penetrated the wall of unchallenged discrimination. We lived in a segregated world, and we simply didn't mix. The only opportunities open to the "Negros" in 1960 were cleaning and menial jobs. Their families lived on the other side of the tracks.

I didn't even see black people except our cleaning lady. They simply served us which seemed like a form of slavery. Our black people were relegated to a much lower standard of living than the white people because southern Indiana was more 'southern' than Indiana. This was 1962, right after Selma and Rosa Parks. Prejudice and segregation were still such an inherent part of our world that it was just business as usual. We assumed this was just the way life would always be. We didn't even recognize this as a problem because we weren't the ones suffering. We simply didn't see it. They seemed to have accepted their lives of quiet desperation.

Mattie's challenge was to cross the color line, walls that seemed impenetrable. She was the experiment whose time had come. She accepted the challenge of being the first black teacher in an all-white school, my school, before desegregation. Mattie bravely entered our school under the critical eyes of her administrators, facing insurmountable odds and prejudices. The county administrators made it perfectly clear to her that if she failed, they would never hire another "Negro" to teach in an all-white school again. Mr. Wiseman, our school principal (aptly named) was truly a wise man who fully supported Mattie through her difficult challenges.

Mattie blazed the trail with her pioneer spirit. As our 6th grade English teacher, she waltzed her way into our hearts with grace and charm. She inspired us in ways no other teacher was able to at Harper Elementary.

After a few years of teaching, her childhood

dream of living in a "white house" was within easy reach. Both she and her husband, William, were teaching school and they had the means to purchase a home.

However, Evansville at that time had an unwritten rule in real estate that Hwy 41 was the dividing line between races. Blacks were simply not allowed to buy property on the other side in the white neighborhoods.

After she gave us a glimpse into part of her challenges. One of her young students, Bob Zimmerman, told his parents that Mattie wanted to buy a house close to our school but couldn't because of the unwritten real estate rule.

Unbeknownst to Mattie his parents were looking for another house and told Bob that Mattie could buy their house. Mattie and her son Kori still own the house to this day. Another wall that Mattie waltzed through.

Several years later Mattie went on to get her master's degree in education administration and became the Principal of Harper Elementary. After many years she retired from Harper. Some of her former students donated the funds to refurbish the auditorium which is dedicated to her. This was a perfect way to honor the one who gave us a voice when we were young. "Questions, Comments or Complaints?"

Mattie Miller today

TABLE OF CONTENTS

Mattie shows the power of one

CHAPTER 1:

The Power of One

"Please believe in 'The Power of One'. One person can make an enormous difference in the world. One person - actually, one idea - can start a war, or end one, or subvert an entire power structure. One discovery can cure a disease or spawn new technology to benefit or annihilate humans. You as ONE individual can change millions of lives. Think big. Do not limit your vision and do not ever compromise your dreams or ideals."

~Iris Chang

"Once there was a man walking along the beach after a storm. He noticed that there were hundreds of starfishes forced onto the sandy beach. He also noticed in the distance a young boy bending over and then throwing something into the ocean. As the man approached the young lad, he realized that the boy was throwing starfish into the ocean.

"Why are you doing this son?" he asked. The boy replied,

"These starfish will die in the heat of the sun if I don't throw them back into the water."

The man smiled with a smirk, "There are way too many here for you to make a difference." The young boy reached down and picked up another starfish and gently flung it into the ocean saying, "I made a difference for this one!"

I was the tender age of twelve when Mattie came into my life and "gently tossed me back into the ocean of acceptance, validation and respect". She took my troubled energy and directed it towards dreams that I didn't know I had lying dormant.

We were mesmerized by her soft sweet southern voice. Her demands for excellence generated confidence and spoke empowerment into our lives. She gave respect in a way no other teachers did. Her firm and loving strength demanded respect and we gladly gave it.

Mattie brought out the best in all of us as she treated us like young adults. This was unheard of in 1962. Her influence sparked our dreams that fueled the direction of our lives for years to come.

She taught us how to get through invisible barriers by her example. She talked to our spirits which had nothing to do with color or age. We spoke spirit to spirit.

How she touched children's lives through words, examples and emotions ushered in the foundations for success.

Mattie spoke to the maturing part of us without criticism. She respected not only who we were but who we were going to become.

She "turned on" our individual drives, instincts, desires and dreams. She set the pace but always respected our speed. Our interactive education was inspiring and engaging. We were experiencing life as budding young adults right there in her classroom.

Her passion pierced our barriers; her love penetrated our hearts. She gave hope to our spirits. Her lessons immersed us into our souls as we learned new ways to communicate. We got infused with her wisdom along with learning life's lessons out of a book.

This spilled over into our relationships with each other. We were sharing and bonding as classmates. This particular little act of listening came after she put her caulk down, crossed her arms and said "Questions, Comments or Complains" while directing our lives at the end of each class.

This unique method was the most valuable part of her curriculum. Her teaching technique of giving us the last 10 minutes of each class to hear what was important to us. During this time, she fed our aspirations, dreams, and desires. This is when we bonded and explored each other's lives.

Every day the comments flew out of our minds. No matter what the subject was. This opportunity to interact with each other literally created a loving classroom environment. For instance, Randy was reading *Mein Kampf, by Adolf Hitler* and explained what the Nazi's had done. It was obvious that he was quite shaken by this travesty. His love and compassion for the Jewish Germans gave us a deeper look into his heart. We began to treat Randy differently.

We didn't realize at the time that she was redirecting our raw energy. I had such an inquisitive spirit that I was labeled as a "chattering troublemaker". Mattie recognized the difference between a rebellious and a playful spirit.

She had the patience to deal with my personality. My other teachers didn't know what to do with me. It was easier for them to be impatient with me. They would resort to calling me "grizel" to get me to shut up. Mattie's approach was to reframe me as a bright student which inspired me to excel.

I went from being a distracted student in school to an exemplary one. She shocked my parents when she told them that she wished she had an entire classroom of students like me.

I went from an average C to a straight A student in a very short time. Rather than feed my "at risk" behaviors, she gave me a new beginning by appealing to my emerging adult. This became apparent to me as I worked tirelessly to please her.

She helped me redirect my restless energy and I discovered my talent as a journalist and writer. She reframed me and my talents by breaking down my barriers. My traumas of not being accepted and the lack of good relationships diminished my self-confidence and drive to shine. Mattie became my inspiration in many ways that I needed at such a tender age.

She was more of a life coach than an English teacher, as she didn't give much attention to the immature part of us. She spoke to our strengths, dreams, and future. Her love and passion was our guiding light.

Mattie challenged us to accomplish our goals and dreams by not allowing barriers get in our way. She literally brought life into our lives with her words, expectations, and high standards. I was this little girl who was inspired to be successful in many different roles as a student, journalist, teacher, businesswoman, mom, and influencer.

She was helping us establish attainable realistic goals. She treated us like little adults looking for our own path. She taught us how to get through the invisible barriers by her example.

We communicated spirit to spirit as we absorbed her wisdom, lessons, and experience. This is how we could cross cultural barriers by blending in respectfully. We learned how to open new doors to new worlds.

Mattie's soul and character infused a "can do" attitude into our lives. Her humble beginnings molded her like a refiner's fire.

Mattie grew up outside of the city on the other side of the tracks. She lived in a 2-room shack with no running water, a wood stove for heat, no indoor plumbing, a stinky outhouse 500 feet from the house and kerosene lanterns for lights. They had to chink the gaps in the structure to keep the wind and snow out.

She was born in Tennessee in 1932 and raised in Alabama. They were not allowed to do things the white kids could do. For instance, they had to go to Kentucky just to get in the movie theatre. They weren't permitted to wear shorts, smoke, or drink. She felt this discrimination later as a young adult.

Since they had no car, they walked everywhere they went. Her family needed to walk 10 miles one way to church every other Sunday. They had a rotating pastor who served 2 churches, one of which was in her neighboring town.

Every Wednesday after school Mattie and her sisters went to their church a few blocks away, for a mid-week evening worship service. Afterwards they had to walk in the dark 10 miles home.

Her mother's warm loving hugs and kisses made life so much easier to deal with. Her mother made life sweet and bearable. Her home was filled with love and peace. Squabbling was taboo in their Christ filled home.

Mattie used her humble experiences to make her better not bitter which exemplifies the adage: "It's the 'I' in bitter who decides to become better." Mattie spent many hours daydreaming about someday living in a "white house".

Her little world was shattered when she was only 5 years old. Her mother lost her life from an infected dog bite leaving a big hole in their family. This was 1937. Now she was forced to grow up tougher and faster. Her circumstances created in her a Christ like charity that only tough times and love could create.

Her compassion spilled over into her teaching career. As our English teacher she taught us how to take our thoughts, problems, concerns, opinions, and issues and put them onto paper.

Writing became a source of journaling that expressed our emotions, problems, solutions, dreams, and desires so we could see ourselves and our true potential.

William & Mattie Miller

She truly invested herself into our lives and that was "Mattie Magic" to us.

We knew how much Mattie cared about us. The other teachers didn't seem to care or at least we didn't feel it. Mattie took to heart the adage, "No one cares how much you know until they know how much you care."

Junior high is a rite of passage between being a child and an adolescent. This is a tough time for most because they are no longer little kids and are not yet adults.

Our other teachers spoke to where we were, not where we were going. Mattie was different. She spoke to the leader in each of us. She was more of a coach for us because she saw our potential.

She gave us tools to succeed by teaching us to think for ourselves. This is when we recognized our own skills and talents. Her expectations for us bred confidence, drive, and the will to thrive.

Her belief in us gave rise to new dreams and opportunities that we still talk about today. She set the environment for discovery and exploration that paved the way into worlds of possibilities. She was the wind beneath our wings. She honored each of us individually as she brought out our best qualities. She expected us to be all that we could be. She imparted an eternal call to each person to reach their own destiny.

She demonstrated to us that she was a "can do" woman who saw the opportunities hidden inside obstacles. She even paved the way for her own husband William to teach in another all-white school, crossing the color line and making the difference.

Mattie gave us the tools and perspectives to see into other worlds and cultures beyond our own. Young people learn to make serious decisions and inner vows at a tender age.

Suddenly the most important thing for me was my vow to follow Mattie's grace in waltzing through walls of uncertainty. Mattie reinforced the concept of us taking action to establish our own high self-esteem. She taught us that others will be more than happy to take us down a couple of notches. She prepared us to fight our own battles in order to succeed and accomplish our dreams and goals.

Words, examples, and emotions instinctively usher into our lives a foundation for success or failure.

She taught us to face our fears and take the road less taken. She introduced to famous poets like Robert Frost's *Road Less Traveled.*
"...Two roads diverged in the woods, and I took the one less traveled and that has made all the difference." by Robert Frost.

We didn't see barriers. We didn't see the walls. We went beyond perceived limitations while we opened our lives with a transparent heart.

I know for me personally that Mattie instilled in me a confidence and resolve to care for the broken hearted while defending the underdog. Her example of letting us teach her while she listened to us elevated us with a "can do" attitude and vision for success in whatever we chose to do.

This indirectly proclaimed liberty to those who were held hopelessly captive to the challenges of life. Mattie's Christ-like spirit and Godly womanhood lifted our spirits that otherwise would be on the shaky ground of insecurity.

Mattie was a portal that God flowed through in order to grace us with the love of Jesus even though she never mentioned God or the scriptures.

The Bible describes love as patient and kind. Love doesn't envy. It doesn't boast. Love is not proud. Love doesn't dishonor others. It's not selfish. It doesn't get easily angry. Love doesn't keep a record of wrongs. It doesn't delight in evil but rejoices with the truth. Charity is the pure love of Christ.

I Corinthians 13:4-8

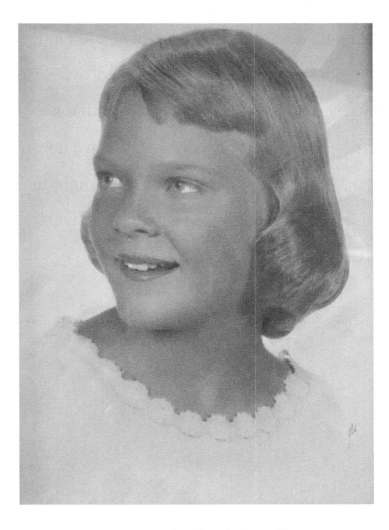

Young Susie Grizzell

CHAPTER 2:

My Life Changed in Sixth Grade

"There is nothing in a caterpillar that tells you it's going to be a butterfly."

~Buckminster Fuller

I clearly remember my first day in sixth grade English class. I entered Mattie's classroom to find to my surprise a black woman. Our parents were concerned and upset that a black woman would be teaching their children. We were intrigued. She was so beautiful that she was easy to watch.

Walking was more of a waltz for her. Her clothes were impeccable, her smile warm and friendly and her voice was musical. She was easy on our eyes and ears. It was clear to us that she believed in herself. Her confidence and posture brought the best out in us.

That's not to say that she didn't demand our best. She expected us to be all that we could be as she imparted joy to make our lives rich. She saw no barriers. We didn't see them either. She rose to the occasion! Hence, waltzing through walls.

At the end of each class, she stopped ten minutes early, put her chalk down, walked to her desk, crossed her arms and said, "The last ten minutes are yours." With a pause she smiled and said, "Questions, comments or complaints. The floor is open. You can talk about whatever you chose to talk about but make it one at a time." We were in shock. No one wanted to hear what us kids had to say.

Adults expected kids to only receive information because they really didn't think that we could teach them anything of value. Mattie changed all of that. She valued our thoughts and ideas. Mattie encouraged our little voices. Slowly we began to speak. She actually listened!

During this time my little world as a 12-year-old opened. I became aware of other's struggles, fears, insecurities, and interests. We explored each other's dreams, visions, feelings, aspirations, and talents as we discussed freely what was important to us individually.

We began to exchange ideas and concepts with each other as we explored each other's world. Thus was the beginning of our bonding as a class while we began to work on our interpersonal communication skills.

We began to interact with each other on an entirely different level. This mix of social interaction was so spontaneous and natural that it was easy for us to excel in her class. It was as though she pulled the adult out of us.

We interacted with Mattie in a much different manner as well. We felt her as a friend but saw her as our teacher. She encouraged us to make the leap into adulthood as if to say "come on over, you can do this. You can be responsible for your own education, actions and future."

She threw out the age-old practice of feeding information for the sole purpose of testing our ability to regurgitate it on a test. Her teaching style was so unique. She encouraged our voices. She drew out our goals and dreams. She cared that we had a practical application to the course material. We learned how to apply what we were learning to prepare us for our next level of education and development.

She called us up to a higher standard. She literally spoke into our lives like we were young adults. She captivated our attention in an atmosphere that challenged us. She used her English lessons to help us organize our thoughts and put them in writing. The practical skill produced excellence in expressing ourselves which spilled over not only to other classes but to our personal lives. We blossomed into inspired confident students with a can-do attitude.

She reinforced the concept that no one will think better of you than you do of yourself. So you think better of yourself. to begin with because others will almost always take you down a couple of notches. She promoted us to define our identity. This grew our confidence and self-esteem. As we opened our young innocent hearts, she related to us on our level as she explored our world with us.

These conversations sometimes extended to after school where Mattie became a counselor for many of us. Mattie knew exactly how to direct our undisciplined energies. I was known as the kid who wouldn't shut up. I was the class' social butterfly. I did like to talk and now I could be heard.

Needless to say, I couldn't wait to get to her

class each day. I was so intrigued and felt so grown up. Little did I know that she would change my life forever!

Some of my other teachers didn't share Mattie's appreciation for what I thought, believed, or dreamed. She made it much easier for me to interact with my other teachers.

Some even went so far as to insult me in front of my class by calling me a slurred version of my last name. "HEY GRIZEL!", as the shop teacher hurled a chunk of wood at me and almost hit my head.

Teachers back then could do anything they wanted. This hot-headed teacher was out of control. It was rumored that he took some of the grade schoolboys' downstairs to the boiler room to smoke cigarettes with him. Despite this we still had respect for him.

Our history teacher, Percy O. Laughlin, would rant and rave as he taught. He scared us with his passion. However, we saw another side of him the day he tearfully shared that President John F. Kennedy had been shot.

Home Economics was an interesting experience with Olive Hawlick. We never knew from day to day if she was going to live past that week.

Art was different. Robert Schmitt was an interesting teacher. It was the last class before lunch and sitting next door to the lunchroom we could smell freedom cooking.

Math was comical as we watched our teacher, Clyde Robinson, doze on the job. He looked like he was going to keel over at any moment. We thought he was well into geezer-hood.

Music class also helped us get through the day. Our teacher, Eulalie Blech, was a fun teacher who opened our gift of singing. As a group we lost our intimidation to sing as we harmonized as a class. She was a great teacher who made sure we learned all the

American patriotic songs. Even the folk songs still ripple through my memories.

The most fun teacher was our science teacher. Mr. Merchant made science come to life. For instance, one of the questions on an exam was, "Where is the observatory located"? One of the wrong multiple-choice answers was, "Grizzell's basement", my basement. We all laughed.

He was a very interesting teacher. He traveled to India one summer to teach the science teachers. He came home with very colorful stories instilling in us a very deep love of India.

Then there was Mattie. What a lovely mix of grace, beauty, and love. I vividly remember my first personal encounter that changed my life forever. Early in the school year we were given a 3-day assignment to prepare for a presentation to our class.

Of course, I procrastinated as usual. I was too busy doing my own thing. To make matters worse I was mildly dyslexic. I really didn't like to read out loud.

Mattie assigned me Rudyard Kipling's poem "IF". Unbeknownst to me this was one of her favorite poems. The first day of presentations I had to go to the front of the class to read "IF". I was unprepared and nervous. I had not even read the poem.

I stumbled through the presentation. When I was done and walking back to my desk, I heard the words that still ring in my ears today. "Well, Susie, there's one thing I can say about you. You sure do know how to think on your feet!" "IF" became my motto through life.

This was a pivotal moment for me. What she said to me was that she recognized that I had not done my homework. She honored me by calling me by my first name. Mattie validated me in a way no other teacher had ever done before.

I was already ineffective in my communication skills. I didn't stand a chance to change my reputation because the teachers would prep each other about me. I was infamous for talking too much. They

46

didn't like me, and I didn't like school. Mattie changed this when she treated me with respect. I worked hard to please her with my work. It paid off handsomely.

I went from being a C student to a straight A's. In the process of trying to please her, I discovered a whole new world that is still with me today. I made an inner vow at age 12 to do for minorities what Mattie had done for me.

I was inspired, full of confidence and excitement. I was so determined to please her with my writing assignments that I would stay up late at night crafting masterpieces.

As a result of Mattie's mentoring, I launched a career in journalism. In high school I became the editor of our school paper, The Prophet, while working for The Evansville Courier Journal as a teenage correspondent.

For my senior research writing project, I chose "The History of the Black Church in America". This paper not only prepared me for college, but it opened the door for me to feel comfortable attending black churches with a welcoming response.

I loved journalism so much that I pursued my career at Indiana University Ernie Pyle's School of Journalism. Ernie Pyle was a foreign correspondent during WWII.

Ernie would go to the front lines and relay the perspective of the soldiers. This was a venue that no other reporter would consider. He won the Pulitzer Prize for foreign correspondence journalism in 1944 reporting from France, Italy, and North Africa. This bravery cost him his life in Japan when hit by enemy gunfire in 1945.

I caught the bug of being a foreign correspondent. Mattie gave me a glimpse into another side of life that most people don't get to see.

My creativity soared. I saw something unusual in my first month in college and created a news story. The Editor gave me a byline on the front page of the school's newspaper. In those days having a byline was like being an editor. After college I would search out opportunities to write.

Fast forward to January 15th, 1993, I heard about a Martin Luther King rally that the KKK wanted to sabotage in downtown Denver, Colorado. I heard that it was going to get ugly, and I wanted to be right in the middle of it as a journalist. Armed with a press pass from the Latino radio station, the disc jockey and I drove right into the crowd to get as close as we could get.

My love of journalism seemed to always put me in the right place at the right time. Many said that I had a nose for news. While I was in high school, I got the opportunity to meet Governor Romney while he was running for

President. Even though I didn't get to write a story about his campaign, I did get my picture taken with him at the Press Conference.

Mattie Miller

CHAPTER 3:

The Teachable Teacher

"Except ye be converted, and become as little children, ye shall not enter into the kingdom of heaven. Whosoever therefore shall humble himself as this little child, the same is greater in the kingdom of heaven."

~Matthew 18:3-4

While writing *Waltzing Through Walls* we called and interviewed Mattie to get the recipe for her "secret sauce". Yes, I call my beloved teacher regularly. Many of her students still keep in touch with her for decades.

"Mattie, how did you learn your teaching skills?" I asked.

Mattie responded, "I don't know. It was just there. It was automatic." Then after a short pause she exclaimed, "Oh, I know! I experienced this with my own high school English teacher. This is how she taught us. It was just natural for me to do the same".

During this interview Mattie shared her fears of being ineffective not knowing how the kids would receive her. She wanted to succeed so that she could remain teaching and we were her first opportunity.

She let us teach her as she taught us. By allowing us to explain to her things she already knew, we had the experience of teaching her. She was gracious enough to allow us to believe that this was new for her. Hence, the joy of teaching. She appreciated the collective intelligence that emerged when we taught her what we knew. She pulled us up as teachers. This occurred during our "Questions, Comments, or Complaints" time at the end of each class.

When a child contributes to the adult then they feel validated in a way that empowers not only the child but the adult. When investing in others it's a kind of a "paying it forward" dynamic. Teach by being teachable, what a concept.

Mattie gave her heart and excellence to her teaching career. We were blessed to be the beneficiaries. We reciprocated this excellence in our schoolwork, attitudes, and performances.

She fell in love with us, and we adored her. Little did we know that her gift of service to us would follow us the rest of our lives.

Susie and Mattie

2018 Harrison Reunion

58

CHAPTER 4:

Black Like Me

"We may have different religions, different languages, different colored skin, but we all belong to one human race."

~Kofi Annan

Mattie gave us glimpses into her life as she waltzed into ours. She treated us as though we were her kids. We felt like her kids too. We had an instant bond unlike anything I had ever experienced with a teacher. We were her little people. We were there to learn, and she was there to teach.

As we merged our lives, we no longer saw color. She opened our eyes and attitudes about our own local prejudices. Our thoughts of segregation were challenged by this intelligent amazing human being.

She taught us by example that we are all God's children. We knew we were one human family. We also learned by experiencing her life's lessons.

She didn't know what prejudice was because she didn't experience that in her younger years. The blatant prejudices of segregation greeted Mattie as she took on the challenges of this job. Mattie didn't see color, only a bright future and endless opportunities. Her sweet spirit radiated in her work with us.

I got a new perspective of other cultures as I entered Mattie's world. For instance, as an upper middle class white girl I had lots of opportunities to experience a variety of trips. At age eleven I clearly remember summer camp in Tennessee. It felt like we were on a Plantation. We had black servants and aids. I was so uncomfortable with the unchallenged acceptance of distinctive racial division. The white privileged southern girls at camp were oblivious to the "Negros" doing all the work. It seemed that the blacks were invisible to these southern girls since they were raised with this nasty prejudice.

Reading books like *"Black Like Me" and "Soul on Ice"* gave me a rude awakening of the ugliness of racial prejudices.

"Black Like Me" is about a white Texan, John Howard Griffin, who decided to experience life as a black man in 1959. *Sepia* magazine financed the project in exchange for the right to print the first account in a series of articles from his 188-page diary.

Griffin worked with his doctor and dyed his skin black, shaved his head and ventured out across the deep south recording his experiences.

He traveled for six weeks throughout the racially segregated states of Louisiana, Mississippi, Alabama, Arkansas, and

Georgia to explore life from the other side of the color line.

His experiences rang true to what I saw in the Deep South. I could feel what was really happening. Traveling with my family to Biloxi, Mississippi in 1962 validated the horror of prejudices I read about in *"Black Like Me"*.

I also vividly remember as a Sophomore in High School taking my reading assignment with me on another family road trip to Mississippi. While reading *"Soul on Ice"* by Eldridge Cleaver my mother reached into the back seat and snatched my book from my hands.

"Why are you reading such a book," she demanded? Before I could respond, she threw my library book out the window?

"I have a book report due on that book in a week", I explained to her.

"Why would you choose a book like that?" she said in a frantic voice. Her emotional outburst surprised me. I felt like I was trapped between two worlds. I was quickly preferring the black world. I felt relief as dad turned the car around to rescue my book.

When we got to Mississippi I was appalled to see "White Only" markers for restrooms and drinking fountains. How were the black people supposed to drink from a water spicket or go to a public bathroom? I was so horrified that they were expected to tolerate the injustice of not being able to use the facilities.

While writing Waltzing Through Walls, my co-writer who grew up in Mississippi in the 1950's informed me that each place of business had 2 rest rooms for women and 2 for men. At the top of the doors read, "Colored Women Only", "White Women Only", "Colored Men Only", and "White Men Only". There were also separate drinking fountains with colored and white markers as well.

On another occasion we flew into Williamsburg, Virginia to see the birthplace of our country. At breakfast one morning I sent my undercooked eggs back to the kitchen.

Low and behold when they were done a black man brought my plate. "Thank you, Sir," I gratefully smiled. As he was on his way back to the kitchen my grandmother glared at me and demanded, "Never address a black man as Sir!". This attitude was a normal part of life, and I was sick of it.

At a young age I made an inner vow to reach out to other people suffering from prejudices and emulate what Mattie had done for me.

Therefore, as a teenager I got involved in our church's inner city Outreach Ministry. Our all-white church was located downtown which was gradually becoming a black neighborhood.

We invited these black children to our Saturday morning ministry. They were so excited that we wanted them. Many of them enrolled in our Bible School and a variety of other activities. I experienced the sweetness of their families. Their flavors of joys were delicious and really touched my heart. I began to feel their joys and sorrows.

Their element of freedom was fascinating to me. They were happy in their own community as they thrived in their segregated world. Their freedom was intoxicating.

I made it a point to enter their community and they warmly received me. The first thing I noticed was that I was immediately accepted. Their world was so complete as they accepted each other unconditionally. I felt warm and welcomed as one of them. Because of some of the friends I made, I became the first white girl in the Junior Division of the NAACP (National Association for the Advancement of Colored People).

After experiencing Mattie, I often entered other cultures and was warmly received by them. I would frequent cultural events and associations in order to make connections.

Eventually opportunities arose where I

would be invited into their lives. This process took time.

There seems to be a vibrational connection that brings a feeling of belonging. Mattie opened cultural concepts that broke down barriers to hard core prejudices. This allowed us to enter her world while returning to our own with a changed perspective.

We don't always see the influence or impact we have on others in different cultures. One ripple can make a lasting difference, good or bad. Prejudice is instrumental in locking up a child's creative potential. Acceptance and love unlock these talents.

Mattie did this for us and we did that for her. As we treat each other like we are family then we allow a bond that knows no culture or skin color. The bond is in appreciation.

She came in to appreciate our culture without losing her own which made us more intrigued by this whole experience. The beautiful part of this is that it was different for each of us based on our life's experiences and aspirations.

We learned that we really are the same no matter what our ethnicity and cultures. When we truly engage with others and embrace their uniqueness, we realize that we are one human family with similar wants and needs.

Generally speaking, we aren't truly listening to others outside of our own culture. Prejudices cause us to look through a filter that causes us to not really hear one another. Therefore, we don't understand each other.

When I saw the movie, *"To Sir with Love"* as a teenager it fueled the inner vow I made in Mattie's class. Sidney Poitier played the role of a black high school teacher in London. He changed the direction of education in his white troubled students when he treated them with love and respect. He won their hearts and spoke truths to help them prepare for their future. This opened up opportunities for them to grow up and accept responsibilities. This is what Mattie did for us.

I was so inspired after watching the movie that I wanted to impact someone else's life. The next day I went to work with my father. I was so determined to help someone and make a difference.

Not knowing how to do that, I walked the streets downtown and discovered an elderly couple sitting on their porch. They invited me into their house. When I saw the disarray, I was humbled. It quickly became obvious that they needed help. They had a walk-through house that sunk into the ground. The back part of the back porch had a dirt floor. They were so elderly and disabled that they couldn't clean.

They didn't have good lighting in the front of the house. It hadn't been cleaned since who knows when. I joined forces with the student council from our school and the student council from North High School and we put together a workday for this couple. Two weeks later we descended upon them to paint and clean their house. We brought in food, and we all ate together.

Since I was a youth reporter, I took pictures and wrote an article in The Evansville Courier Journal, our local newspaper. We were a Godsend to them. This retired preacher and his lovely wife were so appreciative that a group of high school students would spend a day of their time helping them.

Susie and "Charlie" the Iguana,

in Puerto Vallarta Mexico,1991

"THE NIGHT OF THE IGUANA" movie set

CHAPTER 5:

Multicultural

"A multicultural society does not reject the culture of the other but is prepared to listen, to see, to dialogue and, in the final analysis, to possibly accept the other's culture without compromising its own."

~Reuven Rivlin

Mattie opened a door for me to become multicultural. Her introduction into her culture opened my inquisitive mind. Also, my dad took us on "vacations'' after dinner at night with slide shows from other countries. I realized that I had a world to explore. My experiences became an intoxicating joy as I explored other cultures.

My work with ethnic populations continued when I moved to Colorado in the early 1970's. The Mexicans were discriminated against because they couldn't speak English and were treated like migrant workers. Even their children were categorized as migrants.

I became actively involved in establishing an alternative school with Dr. Crocker, Dr. Williams and Dr. Baker, professors of Philosophy and History at Colorado State University.

The goal of this alternative school was to remedy the discrimination of all children and provide a successful learning environment that included disadvantaged kids. Many of them had already dropped out of school because they didn't speak English and there was no effort to teach them.

These kids felt the isolation and unchallenged prejudice as foreigners. The number one goal of De Silio School was to bring these multiple cultures together while meeting their social and educational needs.

Juanita, a 6-year-old Hispanic student, won my heart over as she playfully and unexpectedly jumped onto my shoulders at school one day. At that moment she literally thrust me into her world. I became Mexican. I fell in love with the Mexican people as a teacher's aide at De Silio School. I studied

Spanish so that I could teach them English and talk to their parents.

My life as a Mexican continued during my "divorce-moon" from my husband. This is when I met John Patrick Sterlini, the only Scots Irish, Italian, wetback that I ever met.

He offered me the opportunity to help him create a business in Mexico. They wanted me to be thier American connection. I became an associate in the advertising brokerage company, Sarmientos and Associates, in Mexico City.

Here I was a single mom with a 5-year-old daughter. This risky experience gave me the courage to start my own business in Colorado as I lunged out on my own.

I made so many elite connections in Mexico and the United States that I was invited to the White House briefing to the lobby for NAFTA.

I fell in love with the Mexican people during my stay in Mexico. Their family life was united and invested in each other. Adult children stayed home until they got married. Family was priority above their work. Family included their neighbors and community. They were warm and friendly, kissing each other on both cheeks.

I learned very quickly that I needed to get to know their family, without this they wouldn't do business with me. As I introduced myself, I would get a snicker or smirk. Unbeknownst to me, my last name "Thorpe" was pronounced "torpe", which means "clumsy" in Spanish. This turned out to be a blessing because they didn't forget me. They remembered me with a laugh which was good for business. I saw a connection between the Mexican women and the Arabic women with their male dominated cultures.

My life as an Arab was equally unique. When I lived at Mercy Farm, Terry Redan and I went to Colorado State University to start a Bible study. We instantly became friends with the Arabic women who attended there. We were trying to bring them to know Jesus and they were trying to proselytize us to their Muslim religion.

We became great friends as we explored each other's world. We were teaching them English, and they were teaching us Arabic. Themena invited me to her apartment. I felt like I was in Saudi Arabia. Their wall hangings were like nothing I had ever seen. Their music was equally foreign to me. Then she served me Arabic coffee which was about 1/3 sugar and 2/3 expresso. She left me alone with the music blaring. Upon returning, she asked me if I felt different. "The only thing I felt was a rush from the Arabic coffee".

Their hearts opened to us when we were eager to learn Arabic. The main thing they loved about America was our freedom. I was so fascinated with their culture that I delved deeper into their world by reading *Princess*.

Princess was written by ghost writer Jean Sasson to protect this woman from backlash. This true story is about the good and bad life beyond the veil in Saudi Arabia. This Princess escaped Saudi Arabia after the royal family discovered that she was the one exposing life as a woman in Saudi Arabia. The book was sobering and frightening!

In college, I studied about India, their culture, religions, and culinary arts. I love

Indian food. When I can walk again, I want to travel to India and personally experience this culture.

Another country I fell in love with was Greece. My dad gave me the book, *The Greek Treasure, by Irving Stone, a* love story about Heinrich Schliemann and his young wife. He was convinced that the city of Troy really existed. The Greek scholars in 1871 ridiculed his theories. Against the odds he proved them wrong when he placed the crown of Troy on his wife.

My life was a mess on a Hippie commune where I met John, but God has other plans for me. I went to the Navajo Indian reservation trying to catch up with my friend. After my car blew up at "four corners", I was stranded with my dog and a hitchhiker made me feel very uncomfortable. We waited for help and an Arizona highway patrolman stopped to tell me that I shouldn't leave my car because people would be glad to steal it that night. So, then he drove away without offering any help.

An hour later someone pulled over to give us a rite. They were returning from a Campus Crusade for Christ conference in Denver on their way home to Phoenix. They had to put their baby in the front seat, just to make room for us. They shared their lunch and drove me to the White Post Full Gospel Mission outside of Shanto, Arizona.

When I arrived unexpectedly, I found out that my friend had left and wasn't planning to return. Then I felt abandoned. Early in the morning I borrowed a Bible and I went into the desert, and randomly opened the Bible to Luke 15 "The story of the prodigal son" I was the prodigal one. I received Jesus in my heart as my Lord and Savior. I felt like a new person. That afternoon my friend returned, and we left to retrieve my car. I was blessed to find that my car was still there. After we got a hitch on my friend's car, we towed it back to Denver. I left a piece of my heart with the Navajo people.

John, and I both had a spiritual experience with Jesus on the Navajo Indian reservation. John lived on the reservation for over a year, assisting the Navajo pastor. When I returned home, I was a new person looking for a place to grow in my faith.

In 1972 I joined a Christian Missionary Fellowship in Fort Collins, Colorado. This group consisted of young people who wanted to share Jesus with their friends. This group started as a little Bible study. In a short period of time, we acquired Mercy Chapel and Mercy Farm was established.

By the mid 70's we were a lucrative business, selling our produce and pies to support the missionaries. We became a

Christin commune whose sole purpose was to be trained to take "Jesus Christ to the World in our Generation". This was another key to opening the doors to new cultures.

That summer I called Juanita to invite her to church; she came and wanted her friends to join her. This little group grew to be about ten children. I began studying Spanish at night school to communicate with their parents. I fell in love with these children and many of them fell in love with Jesus. This began my love of the Spanish speaking people.

John came to Mercy farm in 1973, a year later we were married.

I became friends with a young Chinese woman who had just moved to Colorado. She was not fluent in English, and we taught each other our languages. We worked together doing laundry in a sweatshop type facility.

She shared with me many things about China, and knowing her opened my heart for the Chinese people.

All these experiences with different cultures made me a Multi-Cultural Christian.

Alumni from 1964

at Harper Elementary

Evansville, IN.

CHAPTER 6:

Mattie Blazed the Trail for Us

"No one will ever think highly of you, so you'd better have a very healthy opinion of yourself because others will take you down a few notches before they even know you."

~Mattie Miller

Junior high is normally a transitional period from childhood to adulthood. Teenagers are no longer little kids nor are they adults. Mattie spoke maturity into our lives with her adult thoughts. That gave us a chance to develop our identity.

As we discovered ourselves, we explored our talents, dreams, and aspirations. The training we received prepared us for life in high school.

Our high school was brand new on the east side of the city. Interestingly enough, the students from our little feeder school became leaders in this new high school. Mattie's impact prepared us for this new adventure.

Mattie blazed the trail for us to follow with her sage wisdom and fearless example. Her influence instilled in us leadership qualities that inspired us to go into competitive environments. We become leaders in sports, journalism, cheerleading, academia, class speakers, theatre, debate, school government and much more.

Many students recognize her effort to prepare us for our individual future.

For instance, Mattie pulled Don "Donnie" Rice aside one day after school. He was one our most popular classmates. Everyone loved him. When asked as an adult about how Mattie changed his life, Don responded quickly, "That's easy, she saved my life! I wasn't very concerned about school. She noticed that I was excelling in sports and popularity but not in academics. One day she pulled me aside and asked to see me after class.

"I thought I was in trouble, but she surprised me. She directed her attention to me while recognizing my sports and popularity. She cautioned me about my future and if I leaned too heavily on these two areas. She felt I needed to be stronger in academics for a well-rounded life because sports do not always provide for one financially.

"She then offered to tutor me after school. I took her up on it. I stayed after school every day to receive her mentoring. She put me on a sound course, and I've always appreciated it. I have to say that I'm eternally grateful."

She taught by helping us accomplish attainable goals. Mattie treated us like young adults looking for our own path. She challenged us to not let barriers get in our way. Her influence graced our lives with bountiful blessings that we are still realizing today.

In difficult times children can make decisions following their inner vows. Inner vows can be a powerful motivator for good or bad, this will affect how you navigate your life. Sometimes it's a quiet resolve that goes unspoken. My inner vow was very intentional as a preteen and was birthed from my love for Mattie.

Mattie's presence in my life continues to affect me in surprising ways. I had a brush with death in September 2015. As I returned to life, I realized I was unable to continue as

I had before. I could no longer walk and was totally dependent on others to take care of me. I lived in nursing homes, which I renamed "nursing prisons". This was another new culture. Personal choice was replaced by plenty of prejudice. We were treated as though we were incompetent and sent there to die.

I experienced first-hand what conveyor belt care was truly like. Nursing homes are understaffed, and employees are allowed little time for human interaction. Hence, "conveyor care". I felt as though I was held hostage by hospital rules and a cold atmosphere. Feeling like an incompetent burden only compounded the isolation I felt being separated from family and friends.

My free time gave me the opportunity to think deeply about my life and what my future could be. I drifted back to Mattie and her resilience walking into a white world of isolation and prejudices. Growing up in her black community rendered her a little naïve to the prejudices she would experience in the white world.

Her example of navigating the rough waters of fighting the currents of racial prejudices gave me strength. She kept her dignity, posture and character as she dealt with the blatant disapproval all because of the color of her skin.

Mattie showed strength and persevered when other teachers refused to welcome her to their inner circle. At first, they refused to invite her to their lunch table. She chose to eat with the students.

When parents expressed their disapproval of having a black teacher with their children, Mattie remained steadfast in her devotion to her students.

She refused to be sidetracked as she poured her heart into teaching us. She knew she had the approval of Mr. Wiseman, our Principal, and the love of her students.

It's amazing how Mattie's effect on me goes hand in hand with what God is doing in my life today. As I ponder my life totally dependent on caregivers, I remember the "road less travelled".

So here I was in this "nursing prison", reflecting on Mattie's strengths and examples wondering where this road less traveled will take me next.

With no hope of ever getting out of the wheelchair and no longer being able to stand and pivot, I felt trapped, vulnerable, lonely and helpless. I had too much time to reflect and ponder. I've been in seemingly hopeless situations before, but I could walk then.

Answers to prayers worked then and I continued to rely on the Lord now, not knowing what answers He has for me this time.

CHAPTER 7:

My Students Still Impact My Life

By Mattie Miller

"The students at Harper made me the kind of person that I am today. They impacted my life as a teacher and as a woman. However, in the beginning I didn't know how they were going to treat me because they hadn't experienced an African American before. This was before the segregation and civil rights legislation had passed through Congress.

I remember my first day sitting out in the car and crying. I was scared. I expected them to have a bad attitude towards me. I knew I could teach but I didn't know if they would receive me.

Some of the parents actually protested around the school to get me fired. There were parents who would actually stand in the back of the classroom watching me teach. They didn't want a black teacher teaching their kids. Too bad. I was teaching their kids.

Most of it was fear. I don't know what they were afraid of with me. I treated their children the way I treated my own son.

I learned from them like they learned from me. My students taught me that it didn't matter how much money their parents had, kids were kids. They treated me the way they wanted to be treated. I respected them and they respected me.

Kids didn't have a voice back then, but I wanted to change that. One of the things that we don't know as teachers are the things that our students are dealing with. Teach kids good principles and let them make good decisions for themselves.

Some of my students have grown up to be lawyers, teachers, and various other community leaders.

There were so many things that women couldn't do at school back then. So, we focused on what we could do and did it well. It was easy to guide and coach the kids because back then parents made the difference with their students.

The kids were well raised and disciplined. I never had a bad experience where I couldn't go into their neighborhood.

There were pranks pulled on teachers and I made sure I properly warned them to never do it with me. Back then they put thumb tacks in teachers' chairs. "Don't do that to me!" I told them. Talking during the Assembly was also a big no no!. Generally speaking, kids were disciplined at home.

They were taught respect and that spilled over to the way they treated others. I only had to paddle one student. He was using a rubber band as a slingshot with a pin in it and shooting other students in the back while in the hallway.

The principal told me that I needed to paddle him, but I needed to call his parents first. This was in 1962 when we could still paddle students. The young man I paddled is now a successful realtor who has built a lot of homes and still comes to visit me today.

The students did however show partiality towards their fellow students who came from better homes.

There were kids who didn't have much and were discriminated against even by other teachers. The less fortunate students didn't make the cut like those kids whose parents were financially well off such as buying musical instruments.

I wanted to be there every day and it worked very well. The students knew me better than I knew myself. They were my little people. I enjoyed Harper and looked forward to engaging with all my students. I was there for over 30 years.

I feel so blessed that many of my students still keep in touch with me today. In fact, just a few years ago a group of my students invited me to lunch with them. They all gathered around me and celebrated me as their teacher. This warmed my heart in a very special way".

"Just listening to you read Chapter 1 just now brought tears to my eyes," Mattie reminisced. "I was with you as I listened to your recollection and could feel the emotions behind your memories as a student", she said as we gave her a glimpse into *Waltzing Through Walls*. "It just makes me feel so good and I can now go on all night with this excitement".

William Miller 1931 - 2013

The man who danced with Mattie

through all the walls!

CHAPTER 8:

Mattie's Men

William was her husband. Mattie and William met at Tuskegee Institute in Alabama when both were students.

They were well known for winning ballroom dance contests.

Mattie remembers how he could lift her up and move her around the dance floor "We had a lot of fun" Mattie said.

They fell in love and got married in 1953 in Evansville, IN.

Two years later they welcomed their son Kori into their lives.

William & Mattie Miller

William began his teaching career at Central High School in the days of segregation. Later he broke the color line at Plaza Park Elementary in Evansville, IN.

He often teased Mattie because her students seem to love her more.

However, his full story is yet to be told…

Plaza Park Grade School

"In the 7th and 8th Grades, Mr. Miller, Mattie Miller's husband, was our shop teacher.

Mr. Miller was a buttoned- down disciplinarian who taught drafting and woodworking with a sense of cool.

We had the neatest projects where I learned to be a reasonably proficient draftsman, building everything from a Coffee Table to a bookshelf, from a ball ping hammer to a soda bottle opener.

I learned about patience, creativity, discipline and hard work.

But none of this would have happened without Mr. Miller's guidance and tutelage.

I am a better individual, personally and professionally, because of the foundation he helped to build."

~John H. Grizzell

William & Mattie Miller

We can't overlook William and Mattie's devoted son Kori Miller, who has been the most important person in their lives. His dedication to them is a true reflection of his loving family.

Kori Miller, (Mattie & William's son)

"I met Kori Miller- Mattie Miller's son- in high school. Kori was a terrific drummer and I was an aspiring pianist.

Kori and I eventually formed a jam combo with fellow students at University of Evansville- playing tunes from Curtis Mayfield to Parliament-Funkadelic.

Musically, this brief musical epiphany introduced me to a whole new world of soul, funk, and jazz.

I thank Kori for this formative opportunity; it would help to pave the beginnings for a life long appreciation and performance of music."

~John H. Grizzell

Kori Miller

Executive Director of African American
Museum

Evansville, IN

CHAPTER 9:

Mattie's Living Legacy

The following comments reflect some of the myriad of students that Mattie impacted during her life.

"I remember two things foremost about Mrs. Mattie Miller.

First, I thought she was one of the best teachers in the school and I enjoyed her English classes.

The second was a virtual snapshot in memory of the day President Kennedy was assassinated. That memory is 56 years old now, but I think it is still intact.

Word came to us when I was in her eighth grade English class. I remember her standing and looking out the window for some time and when she turned back there were tears in her eyes. I didn't fully appreciate what she must have been feeling then.

It was not until years later that I learned of the wary alliance of the Kennedy brothers with Dr. Martin Luther King Jr. to facilitate desegregation and civil rights in the south and make life better for African Americans.

I probably can't even comprehend what she might have been feeling even today but whereas the brutal assassination of a president shocked all of us it must have had a stronger impact on Mrs. Miller as it called into question the progress the country was making in racial relations.

And of course, I didn't learn until many years later of her concerns about beginning to teach at a young age and moving into an all-white area and what courage that must have taken. But I think most of us were still innocent enough back then that the difference in race was lost on us 13-year-olds. To us she was just one of the finest teachers in the school and one we all liked."

~Doug Harvey

"I Just vividly remember pulling the TVs in the 5th grade classroom and following Kennedy Assassination. Mattie was so strong and was a great calming factor yet there were real tears in her eyes."

~Bill Ellis

There comes into everyone's life, hopefully, that one person that cares about all those in her path – that is Mattie Miller. As a young student I had the honor to have her as a teacher, not just concerning English, but also teaching me life lessons. She has remained a mentor and a friend. I am thankful for finding such a wonderful role model for my life's journey."

~Jon Siau

Women's Equality Day Luncheon Honors Two

Mattie was the first teacher of color at Harper School, then a segregated school in the Evansville Vanderburgh School Corp. She served as principal for Harper for many years and was named Principal of the Year by the Indiana Parent Teacher Association in 2001.

Mattie has been president of the Vanderburgh County Retired Educators chapter and served on the board of the Indiana State Teachers Association and by the National Education Association. She was tapped by the National Education Association for study assignments in West Africa and France.

Mattie has a bachelor's degree from Tuskegee University and holds certifications from University from Evansville and Indiana University. She has taught English, been a reading clinician, a high school guidance counselor, and a middle school principal. Miller has been an adjunct faculty member at Indiana University, University of Evansville, and Ivy Tech State College. She holds an Honorary doctorate degree from the University of Southern Indiana.

~Evansville Courier & Press, August 11, 2019

"Yes, I was in the room when Mattie announced that Kennedy was assassinated, and she broke into tears! Randy Fick came up and threw his arms around her, it was incredible ... I have more stories later.

We had a group that played pickup basketball every Saturday Morning at various locations. I had frequently run into and stayed in touch with Mattie since moving back to Evansville from New York in the mid 80s. Now principle, she had a weekend janitor open the Harper gym for us every Saturday morning for several years.

It was an absolute treat for us "older" guys to have access to such a great gym and especially to be in the same Gym I knew so well and had such great memories and great times in since kindergarten.

Mattie went out of her way to do this for me, one of her more mischievous students years earlier. Mattie was and is simply great!"

~Jimmy Church

HARPER SCHOOL
1956 - 1957

Jimmy Church

Mattie Miller,

"It is with great pleasure and joy to honor my mother in this tribute. She has always wanted to be a teacher and she exceeded that goal by leaps and bounds. Her work in the community has been phenomenal. I want to thank you for acknowledging her and thank God for blessing me with her."

~Your Son, Kori.

"In a difficult time as we are living today with one color mattering over another, we should end the division by loving one another and seeing people rather than color; we're just better together!"

~Mattie Miller

Harper Hornets basketball team.

Harper Hornets basketball team wearing the
new uniform.

Linda Rose, Cindy Cresky, Sally Fulford, Cathy Bossy, Bonnie, Kathy Meier, Annie Weber, Susie Grizzell, Becky Millspaugh, Joyce Cook.

Mattie and her 1965 class reunion.

Class of 1964 in Mattie's classroom.

Photo taken in October 2018.

Part of 1964 class at Mattie's Condo.

Photo taken in October 2018.

Class of 1964 at

Harper Elementary upgraded gym.

Photo taken in October 2018.

Members of class of 1964,

Visiting Mattie in October 2018.

Mattie and former students.

Mattie and former students

Mattie and Bill Ellis

October 2018

Mattie and associates

with EVSC Foundation

In 2018, Harper Auditorium was named after Mattie Miller because she gave us a voice.

New Auditorium named after Mattie

About the Authors

Susie Grizzell Guerra

Susie's life was never the same after her experience with Mattie. English class with Mattie prepared her for a career in journalism. She went on to be the editor of her high school newspaper, <u>The Prophet.</u>

She pursued journalism at Indiana University, then transferred to Colorado State University in 1969. Susie graduated in 1972 with the B.A. in History Education with a teaching certificate. Variety became her spice for life.

After the Vietnam war ended and the protests were over, hippy days left her stranded in the desert. A wayward heart returned her to Jesus and she joined

Christian Missionary Fellowship for the next 8 years.

During that time, she married John Thorpe and was diagnosed with Multiple Sclerosis. M.S. was one of her major life walls. In 1979 their miracle daughter Sarah Ruth Thorpe was born, after life threatening complications.

In 1980 Susie began a new career in Property Management. Three years later she started her own business, <u>Preferred Leads Inc.,</u> a placement agency for property management personnel. This led to starting a business in Mexico before NAFTA.

Susie became a partner with Sarmiento y Asociados (Advertising Agency), in Mexico City, Mexico. In 1987 she earned a Master Degree in Education, M.A. in counseling from University of Colorado. In 1993 she was called to the White House to lobby for Congressional approval of

NAFTA. She married in 1995 with a Peruvian and became the American mom to his two wonderful children, Gisset and Arturo. Unexpected gifts from God.

In 1997 she returned to Teaching at Accelerated Schools in Denver, Colorado.

Another major life wall came after a car accident in 1999 where she received a botched hip replacement that left her in a wheelchair. In 2015 she was rushed to the hospital with a Viral Meningitis with Encephalitis complications where she was in a coma and died. During this death experience the hand of God came to her with a thundering voice saying, "CHOOSE LIFE!"

Being blessed to learn to waltz through walls like her teacher, Mattie Miller, she was faced with more opportunities to waltz through traumas. After two years learning the "nursing prison dance", (nursing home), Susie returned home and began another dance in her wellness journey.

With the help of her therapist Vicki Ariatti, she began rehab and began therapy at Craig Rehabilitation Center with the standing machines and walking in the water exercises, hoping to walk again. COVID became and caused her to face a new wall by having to postpone working out at Craig.

COVID restrictions required her to exit the restaurant through the back door instead of the front with the handicap ramp. She suffered an accident going off the curb in the back of the restaurant breaking both femurs. During the 15-month recovering from this setback she took the time to finish this lifelong dream of writing this book to sing Matties' praises recognizing both our

voices joined in gratitude to our Savior, Jesus
Christ.

Mattie's example has carried Susie through 6
decades of trials and traumas as she too has learned
to waltz through walls.

Vicki Ariatti

Vicki is a Holistic Healer/Traditional Naturopath. In the past 7 years she has been able to help over 700 people break free from their chronic pain and ditch their prescription medications. Her unique methods to get to the root of the problem help those whom doctors have given up on. Vicki helps people in person and remotely. Her clients often tell her how thrilled they are with the results of her work.

Vicki is certified in Cranial Sacral Therapy, Energy Healing and Acupressure. Vicki explains in her Amazon bestseller, *"Hardwired to Heal "* what she's uncovered about how emotional and physical traumas directly impact chronic pain, mental health and diseases. She has a gentle and effective

148

method of clearing and releasing the devastating effects of childhood traumas using Acupressure.

Vicki lives in Colorado, is a proud and very young grandma of 8 grandchildren and 8 great grandchildren. She enjoys singing in the rain, babysitting her great grandchildren and writing books when she's not working.

"But thanks be to God, who in Christ always leads us in triumph, and through us spreads the fragrance of the knowledge of Him everywhere."

2 Corinthians 2:14 RSV

IF

If you can keep your head when all about you
Are losing theirs and blaming it on you,
If you can trust yourself when all men doubt you,
But make allowance for their doubting too;
If you can wait and not be tired by waiting,
Or being lied about, don't deal in lies,
Or being hated, don't give way to hating,
And yet don't look too good, nor talk too wise:

If you can dream—and not make dreams your master;
If you can think—and not make thoughts your aim;
If you can meet with Triumph and Disaster
And treat those two impostors just the same;
If you can bear to hear the truth you've spoken
Twisted by knaves to make a trap for fools,
Or watch the things you gave your life to, broken,
And stoop and build 'em up with worn-out tools:

If you can make one heap of all your winnings
And risk it on one turn of pitch-and-toss,

And lose, and start again at your beginnings
And never breathe a word about your loss;
If you can force your heart and nerve and sinew
To serve your turn long after they are gone,
And so hold on when there is nothing in you
Except the Will which says to them: 'Hold on!'

If you can talk with crowds and keep your virtue,
Or walk with Kings—nor lose the common touch,
If neither foes nor loving friends can hurt you,
If all men count with you, but none too much;
If you can fill the unforgiving minute
With sixty seconds' worth of distance run,
Yours is the Earth and everything that's in it,
And—which is more—you'll be a Man, my son!

Joseph Rudyard Kipling

Made in the USA
Las Vegas, NV
13 October 2021

32221385R00094